taking tea

IMPACTING THE WORLD
THROUGH HUMAN CONNECTION

A 30-DAY DEVOTIONAL

Several years ago, our youngest daughter Rachel embarked on a missionary trip to Africa. She came back with many interesting stories, but the one that intrigued me most was the tradition of "taking tea" every day. When it is time for tea, everyone MUST stop whatever task they are doing and participate in having tea and conversation with whomever they are with at the time.

In our fast-paced world of texts, emails, and social media, I wondered what taking tea in America would look like. Is it possible to adopt some aspect of this wonderful tradition here? I believe so. In fact, I think it is more a question of how we make time in our day than a question of should we make time. Every time we check email, look at texts on our phone, or check our Facebook status, twitter, chat, or whatever our preferred mode of communication is, we sacrifice moments in the present with our loved ones. We check out of the conversation and check in to whatever pops up on our screens.

What is the solution? Am I suggesting that we give up our present technology for human connection? Not at all! I do not believe it has to be an either/or proposition. So how do we take time for connection in our fast paced society?

This book contains some suggestions, but I'm sure there are many more ideas. For this reason, journal pages entitled, "My Recipe for Taking Tea" have been provided to record your thoughts. Get cozy in your favorite spot with a steaming beverage and let's spend time "taking tea" together.

SCHEDULE FACE-TO-FACE TIME WITH PEOPLE

"...for the Lord searches every heart and understands every desire and every heart. If you seek him, he will be found by you." 1 Chronicles 28:9

It is easy to feel forgotten in this world. We are so wrapped up in our own lives. Facebook and other social media sometimes provide a false sense of connection. True relationships take time and nurturing.

I was talking with a mom the other day who was lamenting the fact that she doesn't have an opportunity to see her adult children often because of busyness and distance. This is difficult enough, but she went on to say that even when they are together, her children are on their phones. As a result, she is feeling extremely sad and disconnected from them.

Friends, this is a very real problem in our society. My heart is burdened for her and for others who have confessed something similar. Every time we glance at our phones or take a call, we remove ourselves from the person we are with at the time. We break connection. We lose the present moment with them. It is no wonder so many people are feeling a loss of human connection. It is no wonder we have an epidemic of mental health issues in our communities.

When I'm with others I put my phone away. I confess if it's out I'm tempted to look at it every time I receive a notification. I encourage you to do the same. None of us knows how long we have on this earth. Treat each person as if it's the last time you will have an opportunity for conversation and connection. I guarantee you if we knew these were our last moments with loved ones, we would not spend time on our phones talking with someone else. We would want the people in our immediate presence to know how much they are loved and valued. I encourage you to reach out to a trusted friend today. Determine to get in touch with someone else who may be feeling forgotten. You will both benefit.

PRAYER:

Heavenly Father, help me not to get so wrapped up in my own life that I forget those around me. Thank you that You never forget about me.
Amen

YOUR THOUGHTS

PERFORM AN ACT OF SERVICE FOR SOMEONE

"But when you give to the needy, do not let your left hand know what your right ha
is doing, so that your giving may be in secret. Then your Father, who sees what is
done in secret, will reward you." – Matthew 6:3-4

God calls us to perform acts of service for others. Serving not only benefits the
receiver, but the giver as well. In fact, I personally think giving does more for me th
for the other person. What is even more fun is giving in secret. If we do our action:
in secret, God tells us He will reward us (Matthew 6:3). Giving can be as simple a
sharing a smile or sending a card.

One simple thing I like to do in secret is to buy a hot chocolate for the person
bringing in carts at the grocery store on a cold day. The Starbucks person is alway
very happy to deliver a hot beverage from an anonymous giver. When I'm having a
bad day or feeling anxious or depressed, giving to someone shifts my mood to one
of gratitude for all of my blessings. Personally, I believe that feeling of joy I get is the
reward God is talking about in Matthew.

PRAYER:

Lord, thank You for rewarding us for our acts of service toward others. Help me
to serve as You taught us through Jesus. Amen

YOUR THOUGHTS

BE PRESENT WITH SOMEONE WHO IS GOING THROUGH A DIFFICULT TIME

"Then they sat on the ground with him for seven days and seven nights. No one s
a word to him because they saw how great his suffering was." – Job 2:13

I'm thankful that God has created us in such a way that we can communicate with
words when necessary. Sometimes we want to be there for someone, but are afra
we won't know what to say.

I remember a time when a good friend of mine had a miscarriage. Not only was I
afraid I wouldn't know what to say, but I was pregnant at the time. I was concerned
that my mere presence would add to my friend's grief.

I finally reached out and asked her if she would like some company. She immediate
said yes. I made some brownies (chocolate always makes things better) and went
her house. I prayed on my way over and felt in my heart that I was simply to let my
friend guide any conversation. After an initial hug and whispering the words "I'm s
sorry," I did just that.

We sat outside, ate brownies, and chatted a bit about whatever my friend wanted t
talk about. Most of the time, the only things that could be heard were munching an
the sounds of nature as we sat in companionable silence. When I sensed my friend
was getting tired, I gave her a hug and went on my way. She thanked me profusely
for coming.

If there is someone who would benefit from your presence today, don't hesitate. Sa
a brief prayer, ask God to season your words with salt, (Colossians 4:6) and just be
there for that person.

PRAYER:

Father, thank You for the many times You call on us to simply be there for each
other. If words are needed, You promise to provide them. Thank You for always
being there for me. Amen

YOUR THOUGHTS

_____

_____

_____

_____

_____

_____

_____

_____

_____

_____

_____

_____

_____

_____

_____

_____

_____

_____

_____

_____

_____

_____

COMFORT ONE ANOTHER

"Praise be to the God and Father of our Lord Jesus Christ, the Father of compassi
and the God of all comfort, who comforts us in all our troubles, so that we can
comfort those in any trouble with the comfort we ourselves receive from God."
– 2 Corinthians 1:3-4

I'm thankful that God gave us emotions and that what we are feeling is never wror
A group of us from church led a worship service at one of our assisted worship
facilities. When we arrived, a gentleman was already seated in the room. When I
asked him how he was, he responded, "Not well" and began to cry. He told us his
wife of 68 years had passed away just days before. He then apologized and said,
"Grown men aren't supposed to cry right?" Um... wrong!!! I told him Jesus cried. H
wept over the death of His friend, even though He knew He was going to bring hir
back to life a few minutes later. It is natural to cry over the death of a loved one.

By the end of the worship service, the gentleman was laughing and singing hymns
with the rest of the residents. Through comforting one another, God showed how
turned mourning into rejoicing during even the toughest times.

PRAYER:
Dear Lord, Thank You for being our Comforter. Help us to seize moments to
comfort others as needed. Amen

YOUR THOUGHTS

GOD CALLS US TO BE EARTHLY ANGELS

"For He will command His angels concerning you to guard you in all your ways."
– Psalm 91:11

God sprinkles holy moments throughout the daily moments of our lives. Our daughter Rachel was recently training for a triathlon. One day her schedule dictated a swim in Lake Michigan. I told her I would walk along the beach as she swam. The swim starts a mile from the pier and eventually ends at the pier itself.

Rachel started out and as I watched her I was suddenly gripped by fear. She was way beyond the swimming area. How would boats see her? How would I call out to her if there was danger? She wouldn't hear me. What if she started swimming out into Lake Michigan instead of parallel to the shore? All of these thoughts bombarded me until I started to feel panicked. I prayed, thanking God for His protection, for His shield around her, and for hemming her in. It helped, but I still fe afraid. I decided singing might alleviate my fears. Amazing Grace came to mind so I quietly sang as I walked.

Suddenly, from farther down the beach, I spotted a young girl on a paddle board deliberately making her way to Rachel. She kept pace with Rachel until she was safely in the swimming area. I was so thankful for her. Rachel said she was also comforted by her presence. I wanted to thank the paddle board angel, but I didn't see her again.

Isn't God wonderful the way He answers prayer? He promises to never leave us nor forsake us (Deuteronomy 31:6-8). He shows us His Presence in so many ways sometimes in the form of His earthly angels.

PRAYER:
Father, Thank You for using us to answer each others' prayers. Help us to respond when You nudge us. Thank You for Your peace and comfort and for Your promise to always be with us. Amen

YOUR THOUGHTS

TRULY LISTEN

"Everyone should be quick to listen..." – James 1:19

God gives us many ways to communicate with each other. I was in a coffee shop the other day when a group of people came in and began to talk with each other through sign language. As I looked around the shop, I was struck with the difference between the group of people who used sign language and other group of people who had gathered. Because the group using sign language couldn't hea each other, they were forced to look at one another, intently watching hand signal: and facial expressions. They were completely engaged in conversation. The rest of the tables were filled with people who had their heads down, looking at their phones, replying to texts and social media, while "listening" to conversation. The difference was stark.

The group of people that was signing was laughing and completely engaged with the people around them. The people on their phones were only hearing bits and pieces of the conversation of their friends and family. Every time they looked at their phones and texted, they lost moments with their loved ones. One group left completely fulfilled; the others most likely not.

Determine to truly engage with those around you. Put your phones away, especial if you are sharing a meal or other experience. We can't afford to miss precious time with our loved ones who deserve to feel cherished and valued in our presence. Let's agree to do be more active listeners.

PRAYER:
Father, thank You for Jesus, who was a perfect model of a good listener. Help me to encourage someone today by truly listening to what they are saying. In Your Name. Amen

YOUR THOUGHTS

VIEW INTERRUPTIONS AS "TAKING TEA" MOMENTS

"Do not forget to do good and share with others, for with such sacrifices God is pleased." – Hebrews 13:16

I typically get up early to have my devotions and get some writing in before the day begins. I love this time of the morning. For one thing it's peaceful, and for another, I know I won't get interrupted or distracted by other things that need to get done. If I have to be somewhere early, or my devotion time lasts longer than anticipated, I write later in the day.

One morning I was working on this devotion book, emphasizing the habit of "taking tea" - about the importance of setting time aside for each other. This particular day I found myself feeling mildly annoyed at several interruptions when God reminded me that I was being interrupted by "taking tea" moments. Oops! Here I was writing about the importance of face-to-face connections and feeling annoyed when they were taking place in my life!

God promises when we make time for Him and for the people in our lives, He will make time in the day for everything else that is important. If it doesn't happen, it wasn't important. People should always take precedence over our to-do lists. True to His word, there was unexpected time later in my day for my writing.

PRAYER:

Father, help me to never see others as "interruptions," but as Your children seeking a "heart moment" with me. Help Your children to see You in me. Amen

YOUR THOUGHTS

SHOW HOSPITALITY

"Do not forget to show hospitality to strangers, for by doing so some people have shown hospitality to angels without knowing it." – Hebrews 13:2

My husband and I recently joined a Divine Dining experience put on by our church. The purpose of the event is to get to know others in our congregation we may not have had the privilege to meet yet. As the day grew closer, I grew more and more stressed, concerned that my house would not be as clean or organized as the ladies' homes that were coming over. I somewhat knew the ladies from church and they are known for their organization skills. I, on the other hand, am not. God reminded me that I have other gifts and that the purpose of getting together was for fellowship, not to inspect my home. I finished cleaning and said a prayer for all those coming. At dinner that night I focused on my friends and not on the state of my home. Everyone had a wonderful time and I had an opportunity to fellowship with couples I only see in passing at church on Sundays - a blessing for sure.

PRAYER:
Father, help me to always be willing to share my home with others. Remind me to focus on people, not on what my house looks like. Amen

YOUR THOUGHTS

HAVE A VISION BIGGER THAN YOURSELF

"Where there is no vision, the people perish." – Proverbs 29:18

Be thankful for God's vision for our lives. God says in the above verse that people without vision will perish. This is not always a physical death. Sometimes we are physically alive, but have lost purpose in our lives. As long as we are still here on earth, God has a purpose. Having a vision bigger than ourselves cuts down on anxiety and depression because we are more focused on others than on ourselves. When we help others discover their hopes and dreams, we feel better about ourselves.

PRAYER:

Father, thank You for the dreams You plant in all of our hearts. Show me how to help others discover and use their gifts as well. Amen

YOUR THOUGHTS

BLESS SOMEONE WHO IS GOING THROUGH A CHALLENGING TIME

"Do not use your freedom to indulge the sinful nature; rather, serve one another humbly in love." – Galatians 5:13

Be thankful for all of the abundance in your life. So often we think of abundance in terms of money and possessions, but true abundance is found in our relationship with Christ and in the people we have in our lives. Jesus tells us in Luke 12:14 that life does not consist in an abundance of possessions.

Many people who are rich in material things are poor in the things that matter. They may be going through divorce or may be at odds with their children or other family members. No amount of money or things can make up for the loneliness they feel.

Today, if you are rich because of the loved ones in your life, give thanks. Reach out to someone who may be going through a difficult time and offer your friendship. You will both be blessed.

PRAYER:
Heavenly Father, thank You for the abundance of relationships in my life. Help me to freely share my gifts and time with others. Amen

YOUR THOUGHTS

DOUBLE YOUR JOY AND DIVIDE YOUR SORROW

"Two are better than one, because they have a good return for their labor. If they fall down they can help each other up. But pity those who fall and have no one to help them up!" – Ecclesiastes 4:9-10

There are many who are grieving a tremendous loss in their lives. Maybe you are grieving. If so, I came across a suggestion the other day to find a way to minister to someone else. When we help others, WE ourselves are helped. Jesus calls us to serve. He came not to be served, but to serve (Mark 10:45). Jesus knows that in serving, both the server and the one being served will be blessed.

Serving from a place of grief is difficult, but when we are faithful in this way, we are filled with so much love our heart smiles. In sharing, our joys are doubled and our sorrows divided.

Today, if you are in a dark place, or even if you are not, I encourage you to find someone to bless. I have no doubt you will experience a rebound of joy in your own life.

PRAYER:
Jesus thank You for Your example of service while You were here on this earth. Help me to look for ways to serve and to be a willing servant. Amen

YOUR THOUGHTS

FIND SOMEONE TO SERVE

"In the same way, faith by itself if it is not accompanied by action, is dead."
– James 2:17

Did you know Acts is the largest book in the New Testament? Do you think this is a coincidence? Without the ACTS of the apostles, the gospel would have ceased to exist. God calls us to action.

God tells us that faith without action is dead (James 2:14-17). We can read our Bibles and pray all day long, but if we never DO anything, if we never serve, our faith doesn't mean much. God tells us our words are empty, a resounding gong or a clanging cymbal (I Corinthians 13:1). We can have the greatest faith and knowledge, give all we have to the poor, and offer ourselves to hardship, but if we don't do it out of love, it doesn't mean anything.

Many people are struggling with anxiety and depression today. I'm sure there are many reasons for this, but I believe one of the biggest reasons is we have lost a sense of CONNECTION. Today, find someone to serve, even if it's something as simple as a phone call (texting doesn't count) :), sending a card, or meeting someone for a walk, or coffee. Intentionally reach out to someone. You will both be blessed.

PRAYER:

Father God, thank You for always being available to me. Help me to make time for true connection with someone today. Amen

YOUR THOUGHTS

SHARE YOUR FAITH JOURNEY WITH SOMEONE

"For we are God's handiwork, created in Christ Jesus to do good works, which God prepared in advance for us to do." - Ephesians 2:10

Be thankful that your identity is in Christ. So often we confuse who we are with what we do. If we suddenly find ourselves out of work for whatever reason, we feel like we have lost our identity. I experienced this temporary loss of identity when I left a teaching career to help our adults with unique abilities in the community. I would wake up in a panic at night wondering, "Who am I?" I had to remind myself over and over that I am a child of God, a daughter of the King.

Your identity will never change, no matter what your life brings. You are special because your identity is in Jesus, not in what you do for a living.

Today take a moment to give thanks that you were created in Christ's image and then share this truth with someone else.

PRAYER:

Thank you Jesus that our identity is in You. Show me how I can demonstrate this truth to others. In Jesus' name. Amen

YOUR THOUGHTS

_____

_____

_____

_____

_____

_____

_____

_____

_____

_____

_____

_____

_____

_____

_____

_____

_____

_____

_____

_____

BE CAREFUL NOT TO JUDGE OTHERS

"Do not judge or you too will be judged. For in the same way you judge others, you will be judged, and with the measure you use, it will be measured to you." – Matthew 7: 1-2

I was in the grocery store parking lot the other day when I heard a woman mutter sarcastically, "Just leave your cart there. Nice." She was referring to a young woman who parked her cart next to her car. The young woman overheard and quietly mentioned that she had 3 young children in the car and didn't want to leave them. The cart return was a fair distance from her car.

At this point, the complaining woman's passenger simply offered to return the cart for the young woman and promptly did so. The young mother was very grateful and thanked her profusely.

How much easier and rewarding it is to simply "return the cart" instead of grumbling and complaining about another's behavior. We have no idea what this young mom's journey looks like. Is she a single mom trying to do the best she can? Does one of her children have a disability that makes it unsafe for her to leave the child unattended, even for a moment? Does it even matter why she can't return her cart?

Jesus would have treated the young woman with love and compassion, regardless of her situation. He would have simply "returned the cart" without judgment. Together, let's resolve to reserve judgment for God alone. Only He knows what battles each one of us is facing. Today, simply "return the cart" for someone without judgment. Demonstrate Christ's love for another person and bask in His love and approval.

PRAYER:

Father, thank You for Your reminder to refrain from judging others. Help me instead to love my neighbors, to be an encourager and to shine Your Light wherever I go. Amen

YOUR THOUGHTS

TREAT OTHERS WITH THE SAME RESPECT JESU SHOWED TO ALL THOSE IN HIS PRESENCE

"A gentle answer turns away wrath, but a harsh word stirs up anger." – Proverbs 15 God promises to give us the words we need in the middle of a tough situation whe we remember to ask Him. The key is to ask. James 1:5 says if any of us lacks wisdo we should ask God, Who gives generously to all, without finding fault, and it will b given to us.

I was in the middle of a stressful situation the other day when someone I had just m chose to unleash her fury at me. I was first stunned and then became very defensiv angrier than I remember being in a very long time. I unleashed a bit back at her an then suggested we end the conversation. When we resumed talking, we came to a agreement of sorts and moved on with our day. Unfortunately, I had difficulty lettin the situation go and vented to several friends before I left work for the day.

When I went to my second job for the day, I was finally able to let it go and focus or what I needed to do. One of my friends at this job spontaneously said how happy s was to see me as soon as I came in, how I always make her day. Her words were so soothing and beautiful after the day I had just experienced. Never doubt the powe of what you speak to others - good or bad.

When I left work for the night, however, my anger and hurt returned. I shared the experience with my husband, prayed about it, and felt more at peace, but there was still some residue of the experience with me the next morning. I found myself reflecting on what I could have done differently in the situation. I sensed God impressing on me that my first instinct should have been to offer up a quick prayer, asking for peace, wisdom, and guidance. It would have been better to remain quiet for a few seconds and let God speak through me. I could have asked the person what she needed from me rather than responding defensively. Maybe we could have come to a resolution right then. I should not have talked about the situation wi several other people. If I was still angry, I could have confided in one good friend. I also needed to keep praying in order to let my hurt and anger go.

Our human nature sometimes gets the best of us. I'm thankful that God understand our humanity, offers His forgiveness, and gives us wisdom for future situations. I love how in the above passage God promises to provide wisdom without finding fault.

What situation do you need to let go of today? Don't try to release it in your own power. Allow God to instill His wisdom, love and peace in your heart and move on.

PRAYER:
Jesus, thank You for being a perfect example of how we should treat others - always swift to hear, slow to anger, and abounding in steadfast love. Help me to do the same for all those around me today. Amen

 YOUR THOUGHTS

_____

_____

_____

_____

_____

_____

_____

_____

_____

_____

SHARE YOUR UNIQUE GIFTS

"There are different kinds of service, but the same Lord. There are different kinds of working, but in all of them and in everyone it is the same God at work."
– I Corinthians 12:4-6

There are many kinds of gifts, but the same Spirit who distributes them. I have read the above passage many times before, but for some reason it hit me with intensity and amazement today. Amazement that God would carefully craft us in His image and then thoughtfully consider the specific gifts He gives us.

God considers each one of us - each one of us! Ponder the enormity of that statement. I imagine Him lovingly molding me, creating me when I was still in the womb, as an artist would a masterpiece, marveling over His creation. As a final touch, He custom-designed gifts, unique only to me, and planted a kiss on my head, sealing me with His Spirit. He quietly told me to be sure to use the gifts He had bestowed on me, for there is no one else quite like me, and then sent me out into the world.

He does the same thing for each one of us. No one gift is better than another. We are created to combine our gifts in order to create meaning and beauty in this world. We need ALL of the gifts.

I sensed anew how much God loves us. He must if He puts that much time and attention into creating us in His own image and at the same time, uniquely blesses each of us.

Today, go forth with the assurance that you are loved and use your gifts. There is only one YOU and the world needs what you have to offer.

PRAYER:

Thank You Lord for the care and attention You gave each one of us as You brought us into being. Help me to celebrate my unique gifts, as well as the special gifts and talents of those around me. Amen

YOUR THOUGHTS

LAUGH WITH SOMEONE

"The One enthroned in heaven laughs." – Psalm 2:4

Be thankful for laughter - a simple taste of Heaven here on earth. I hope my funeral is filled with joy.

I saw a picture once that I have never forgotten. The title said simply "Jesus Laughs". In the picture, Jesus' head is thrown back in laughter. His face is full of joy and pleasure. In my imagination He was laughing at something a small child had said, but Jesus may have just as easily found joy simply because He was in the Presence of His Father who loved and cared for Him.

I have often wished there was a verse in the Bible that said simply, "Jesus laughed." In our world full of trouble and sorrow, it is especially important for us to find something humorous that will cause us to laugh out loud.

Laughing is always better shared. When something is funny, often the first thing I will do is look around to see if anyone is laughing with me. When there is, I feel an instant connection with that person.

Today, spend time with family and friends who make you laugh and then share your good humor with those in your path.

PRAYER:

Father, thank You so much for laughter. I look around this world and see evidence everywhere of Your sense of humor. All of the funny insects and animals You have designed are proof of the fact that You love to laugh. You have built the desire to find humor inside each of us. Help me to share the gift of laughter with those around me. Amen

YOUR THOUGHTS

SHARE A MEAL OR A CUP OF COFFEE

"Where two or three come together in my name, there I am with them."
- Matthew 18:20

I love heartfelt chats over a cup of coffee in the morning. One of my favorite things to do with my daughters when they are home is to catch up over a cup of coffee. Before we go to bed the night before, we always set a time the next morning for our coffee chats.

So often we awake in the morning with regrets over yesterday, stress over today's to-do list, or worries over the future. Today think of five people you are grateful for in your life RIGHT NOW - not people in your past, not people in your future. Accept the fact that we can't control all of the events in our lives, but we can choose to be grateful for what we have today.

Go one step further and take time to thank your five people somehow. Send a card. Thank them face-to-face. Make a phone call. Share a cup of tea or a meal. Be Christ's light to someone.

PRAYER:

Father, thank You for precious time with our loved ones and for promising to be in the midst of our gatherings. Help me to be Christ's Light to someone today. Amen

YOUR THOUGHTS

LEARN ABOUT
OTHERS' JOURNEYS

"I have fought the good fight. I have finished the race, I have kept the faith."
– 2 Timothy 4:7

I often need to remind myself to focus on my inner world: on my spiritual walk, health, and things that are in my control. Worrying about what others are doing or not doing, what they think about me or about life in general, only leads to a loss of energy for what I'm being called to do. It is so important to stay on our own paths and accept that others are on their own journeys. I have no idea what challenges others are facing, what inner battles they are fighting.

Judging others becomes a stumbling block in my path. Instead I'm trying to remember to pray for people, send them love, and work on running my own race, on staying the course. It's a challenge for sure, but thankfully God promises to provide what we need in order to stay true to our daily walk with Him.

PRAYER:
Thank You for giving each of us our own unique journeys. Help me to stay the course while encouraging others on their individual paths. Amen

YOUR THOUGHTS

BE AT PEACE
WITH OTHERS

"If the home is deserving, let your peace rest on it; if it is not, let your peace return to you." – Matthew 10:13

Be thankful for the peace we have in Christ.
There will be difficult people in our lives who can steal our peace and joy if we allow it. We have a choice in how we react to others. We can CHOOSE not to allow people to take our joy and peace from us. Knowing others' particular challenges often provides a better understanding of them, even if we don't agree with the way they handle their frustrations and difficulties.

When Jesus sent his disciples out to certain homes, He told them to speak peace over the residents there. If their peace wasn't received, it came back on the disciples. If we do our best to be at peace with others and it's not accepted, that peace will come back on us. What a wonderful promise! We get our peace back, as well as their share; we are gifted with double the peace!

Today, CHOOSE to stay in peace. Continue to do the right thing. Take the high road. Let God fight your battles and be in harmony with each other.

PRAYER:

Father God, thank You for Your Peace. Help me to take an interest in others' lives so I can better understand the challenges they are facing. May I always be an instrument of Your Peace. Amen

YOUR THOUGHTS

_____

_____

_____

_____

_____

_____

_____

_____

_____

_____

_____

_____

_____

_____

_____

_____

_____

_____

_____

_____

_____

LOOK BEYOND PEOPLES' EXTERIORS

"The Lord does not look at the things human beings look at. People look at the outward appearance, but the Lord looks at the heart." – I Samuel 16:7

Sometimes a person appears unapproachable. They may have a harsh look on their face or appear angry or disapproving, but may actually be thinking about something else. They may have people or events in their lives that are causing them deep sadness or worry. Chances are, the look has nothing to do with us. I love this reminder to look beyond the exterior of people.

A simple smile or hello could change their day. Even if they are upset with us, we are called to respond with love and kindness, just as Christ responds to us when we are not being our best.

Choose to smile and say hello to someone who may look unapproachable. You never know how far that simple act of love may go. Be a light in someone else's life. A speaker suggested, "Instead of dimming our lights to appease others who say our lights are too bright, hand them a pair of shades."

PRAYER:

Father, help me to see others with Your eyes and to respond in love to all those I come in contact with today. Amen

YOUR THOUGHTS

6-21-20

Rec'd this on 6-21-20 - I try and apply
this always, but I have had people
say they thought I was unapproachable.
I have been through a lot of trying times
in the past few years. I don't mean to
appear that way, but even after I
have talked to these people - they stayed
their distance from me (and at church)

MAKE SOMEONE'S DAY

"Do not merely look out for your own personal interests, but also for the interests of others." – Philippians 2:4

As we are counting our blessings we are called to bless others as well. God blesses us and then gives us opportunities to bless others. When we share what we have with others, whether it's our time, money, or skills, we can't help but be blessed as well. In fact, most of the time, I am blessed more than the receiver. Sometimes when I'm having a bad day or someone has mistreated me, my solution is to deliberately choose someone to bless. If I can find a way to bless them in secret, it's even better. It's kind of selfish on my part because I know I will be blessed also. The joy I receive from performing an act of service, especially in secret, is overwhelming.

Choosing to make someone's day is so much better than complaining about how bad our day is or how someone acted toward us. I confess I have a long way to go with this, but any progress is good.

Find someone to bless today, especially if you are struggling with something. It doesn't have to be something big. It doesn't even have to cost you anything. You will be amazed at how joyful you feel.

PRAYER:
Lord, thank You for all of my blessings. Please place someone in my path today that would benefit from a small act of kindness. Amen

YOUR THOUGHTS

GIVE A COMPLIMENT

"So God created man in his own image; in the image of God he created them; male and female he created them." – Genesis 1:27

Every single human being is a reflector of God, created in His image. If you ever doubt your worth, and my guess is we all do from time to time, remind yourself that you are created in God's image and nothing about God is "wrong" or "messed up". Yes, we are human and therefore imperfect, but we are also spiritual beings, created for a purpose.

We may find ourselves looking at others differently when we remember that all of us are reflections of our Creator. Take time today to thank God for creating YOU. He loves you just as you are.

Our true beauty lies within, although when we have God's joy and peace in our lives, our outward appearance is affected as well. Think of the times you felt most beautiful: maybe it was on your wedding day; as you marveled at the child you birthed; when you were caught up in work that made your heart soar; or after you performed an act of kindness for someone. It is Love that gives us our beauty. We reflect God when we go about our days doing what we are called to do. Today let your light shine!

PRAYER:
Thank You Creator God that we are all made in Your image. Help me to see You in everyone I meet. Amen

YOUR THOUGHTS

REMIND SOMEONE GOD HAS A PLAN

"For I know the plans I have for you," declares the Lord, "plans to prosper you and not to harm you, plans to give you hope and a future," - Jeremiah 29:11

God calls us to serve others. This truth is becoming more and more evident to me, especially when it comes to my business. I'm learning to ask different questions. Instead of asking how I can promote my business or how I can make income doing what I love, I am learning to ask how Transition Bridges can bless others. How can I best minister to people through my business?

When we ask how we can best serve God and others, God's Peace replaces anxiety and uncertainty. There is a plan and it's a good one: a plan to prosper and not harm; a plan for a hope and a future (Jeremiah 29:11).

PRAYER:

Father God, thank You for the perfect plan You have for each of our lives. Show me opportunities where I can help others discern Your plan for their lives as well. Amen

YOUR THOUGHTS

REPLACE WORRY
WITH PRAISE

"Do not be anxious about anything, but in prayer and petition, with thanksgiving, present your requests to God." - Philippians 4:6

Psalm 139:23-24 states, "Search me O God, and know my heart; test me and know my anxious thoughts. Point out anything in me that offends you, and lead me along the path of everlasting life."

God knows our hearts so well. He wants to take anything that is causing us anxiety - anything offensive- and transform it into thanksgiving and praise. I love that He leads us on a path that ultimately results in eternal life with Him where there will be everlasting peace. God wants us to experience that peace here on earth as well.

Today give Him anything in your heart that is causing you anxiety. Focus on God and on His tremendous love for you. Do something that is an intentional act of praise to our loving God. Say a prayer. Sing a song of praise. Write God a love letter. Take a walk, praising God for all that He has created, including you and those you love. Do whatever reminds you that God loves you with an everlasting love.

Go one step further and pray for others, write them a note of encouragement, invite someone to take a walk with you, or meet up with you for "taking tea" time.

PRAYER:

Thank You Father for Your amazing love! Thank You for knowing my heart so well. Today I give You all that is creating anxiety in my life and offer You praise in its place. Amen

YOUR THOUGHTS

BE GRATEFUL FOR
YOUR GIFTS

"If you're content to simply be yourself, your life will count for something."
- Matthew 23:12 (MSG)

God creates us each in His own image. Do you ever find yourself thinking thought of how you want to be like someone else in one way or another: "Why can't I be more organized like her?" "I wish I was thin like that person." "She has her business figured out while I'm spinning my wheels."

What if we choose to listen to God's Voice over the voices of the world and thoughts in our own heads? I know I'm not the only one who struggles with this. When my thoughts go every which way, it takes great intention and lots of prayer to reign them back in.

God is happy to meet us where we are. He wants you to be you and me to be me. Even people who look like they have it all together struggle with some area of their lives. We are created in God's image and are loved with an everlasting love. Let's choose to listen to His voice over the voices of the world and in our own heads.

Today determine to flood your mind with God's words and His thoughts about you. Treat yourself with grace. You are who God says you are. He says you are His child His friend (John 15:15). You are loved with a greater love than you can ever imagine (Jeremiah 31:3).

God wants us to reach out to others when we feel inadequate. He wants us to ask people how they are thin, organized, figured their business out, etc. and then share our areas of strength and wisdom. He created us uniquely so we can help each other. Apart we are weak. Together we are strong.

Who do you need to ask for help or advice today?
What gifts can you share to help someone else?

PRAYER:
Father, thank You that You have created us to need each other, to share each other's gifts. Help me to share freely what you have given me and to ask when I need help in a specific area of my life. In Jesus' name. Amen

YOUR THOUGHTS

_____

_____

_____

_____

_____

_____

_____

_____

_____

_____

_____

_____

_____

_____

_____

_____

_____

SHARE ABUNDANTLY

"Taking the five loaves and the two fish and looking up to heaven, he (Jesus) gave thanks and broke the loaves. Then he gave them to his disciples, and the disciples gave them to the people. They all ate and were satisfied, and the disciples picked up twelve basketfuls of broken pieces that were left over." – Matthew 14:19-20

Be thankful that God is able to take the little you have and bless others abundantly. I love the story in the Bible of the feeding of the five thousand (Matthew 14:13-21). If you are not familiar with the story, after a day of preaching to thousands of people, it was time to eat. The disciples wanted to send the people into town to eat, but Jesus asked them to see what was available. One little boy offered up his two loaves and five fishes, which the disciples told Jesus was barely enough for themselves. Jesus accepted the offering regardless of their protests, blessed the food, and gave it back to the disciples to distribute.

The food fed all five thousand people, with 12 baskets left over! Amazing! God performed this miracle one other time, feeding four thousand people.

Imagine what an impact Jesus' miracle made, not only on the people served, but on the little boy who willingly offered his lunch that day. Wow! If his mother wasn't there that day he must have excitedly shared with her later what Jesus had done. I wonder if her life was changed as well.

God takes the very little we have and uses it ABUNDANTLY. He wants us to focus on what we DO have, not on what we don't have. He calls us to share with others out of our abundance, promising that everyone served will be blessed.

His message not only refers to our material possessions, but also our Spiritual gifts. We don't always see how the little we possess, or the gifts we have, can be a blessing to others. This is where faith comes in, a belief that God can turn our small offerings into a miracle for others. Be grateful, give thanks, ask for God's blessing on our gifts, and share with others, believing that God will use our offering abundantly. God lacks for nothing.

day, offer your loaves and fishes and watch how God performs a miracle in your e and others' lives as well. Even if you don't actually see what God has done, have ith that He did something amazing. All of Heaven is rejoicing in your offering.

RAYER:

hank You Lord that You can turn even the little I have into something amazing. how me opportunities where I can help others magnify the gifts You have given em. Amen

YOUR THOUGHTS

GIVE THANKS FOR
DAILY BLESSINGS

"God again set a certain day, calling it 'Today.'" – Hebrews 4:7

God gives us glimpses of Heaven each day. When Jesus died, the curtain of the temple was torn in two from top to bottom (Mark 15:38), signifying that we now have access to Heaven through Jesus. The veil between Heaven and Earth is very thin.

The other day the teacher in my classroom put on some music while our students finished their work. One of our students, who is not very verbal, suddenly got up and began dancing while singing in her sweet voice, "I see your true colors shining through. I see your true colors. That's why I love you." The teacher and I quietly joined in. It felt truly magical for a brief few moments.

God turns ordinary events into extraordinary moments when we take the time to acknowledge and appreciate the events and people who make up our daily lives. So often we are so busy counting down the days to some important event coming up we miss the gifts that are right in front of us.

Today determine to truly see all of the beauty that fills our days and take a moment to give thanks. Your day will be transformed into something amazing and beautiful.

PRAYER:
You fill my life with blessings every single day. Help me to acknowledge what I have and give thanks, always. I pray this in Your Son's precious name. Amen

YOUR THOUGHTS

ASK GOD AND YOU WILL RECEIVE

"We do not know what we ought to pray for, but the Spirit himself intercedes for us through wordless groans." – Romans 8:26

God gives us His words when we are not sure how to pray for ourselves or for someone else. There are times I'm at a loss when it comes to praying for those I love. I came across these words in Colossians 1:9-13 the other day:

"For this reason, since the day we heard about you, we have not stopped praying for you. We continually ask God to fill you with the knowledge of His will through all the wisdom and understanding that the Spirit gives, so that you may live a life worthy of the Lord and please Him in every way: bearing fruit in every good work, growing in the knowledge of God, being strengthened with all power according to His glorious might so that you may have great endurance and patience, and giving joyful thanks to the Father who has qualified you to share in the inheritance of His people in the kingdom of light." Paul and his followers prayed this prayer every day from the time they heard about their friends.

I don't know about you, but I would love for someone to pray for me this way every day. When we don't know how to pray, we can also pray the Lord's Prayer or any of the Psalms. Psalm 23 is a favorite of many people. We can pray any of the Scriptures for that matter. The important thing is to pray for one another.

PRAYER:

Thank You Jesus that You taught us the Lord's Prayer as an example of how we are to pray. Thank You for Your Word and for Your Spirit that intercedes for us when we don't know what to pray. Help me to come to You with all of my joys and sorrows and to lay others before You as well. Amen

YOUR THOUGHTS

JESUS LOVES EVERYONE

"For God so loved the world that he gave his only begotten Son, that whoever believes in him shall not perish but have eternal life." – John 3:16

We are loved more than we can imagine.

God loves us so much that He sent His Son Jesus to be a model of how we are to live. Not only that, but He sent Him to die for our sins so that we can have eternal life with Him. If you or I had been the only people on earth when Jesus came, He still would have sacrificed His life. He loves us so much that He would die for any one of us. Amazing!

He calls us to lay down our lives for one another. Jesus came not to be served, but to serve, and He calls each one of us to do the same. Jesus is LOVE personified.

What I am learning on this journey is to set judgment aside for God, and to use my time and energy to love my neighbor. I won't always understand their actions, just as others won't always understand mine. It doesn't matter. What matters is that we love God and love our neighbor, and we acknowledge and appreciate each other's gifts. What matters is that we see our loving Creator in each other. What matters is that we are a light in this world, just as Christ is our Light. Shine for Jesus, friends. Shine for Jesus.

PRAYER:

Heavenly Father, thank You for loving us so much You sent Jesus to be our Savior. Thank You for being our Light. Help me to shine for You each and every day. Amen

YOUR THOUGHTS

art of the proceeds from the sale of this book, Taking Tea - Impacting the World
through Human Connection, will support SEND International. Our daughter,
Rachel, mentioned in the beginning of the book, works for this wonderful
organization.

SEND International is a missionary organization seeking to plant churches
among unreached people groups around the world. They send out missionaries
to areas of the world where less than 2% of the population are evangelical
Christians. SEND seeks to bring hope to the hopeless, and the good news of the
gospel of Jesus Christ to those with the least access to it.

Rachel works for SEND as a Missions Coach. Her main focus is to bring greater
understanding of God's heart for the nations and to heed Jesus' call to spread
His teachings to all nations of the world. She works with people who feel called
into missions and helps them seek God's role for them in His Great Commission.

Rachel also helps to mentor, train and prepare missionaries for the field. She
provides resources to local churches, enabling them to send their missionaries
out into the world.

Your purchase of Taking Tea - Impacting the World Through Human Connection
will result in the changing of many lives.

Thank you!

I would like to take a moment to thank some very important people in my life. This book would not have been possible without my family - for their continued support and encouragement on this journey. Thank you goes to my husband Scott, daughters Heather, Courtney, and Rachel, and son-in-love Ethan, for being my cheerleaders. A special thank you goes to my daughter Rachel for sharing her story of taking tea. This book was born out of her inspiring stories of life as a missionary. A very special thank you also goes to my daughter Courtney - for taking time out of her already extremely busy schedule to make edits and suggestions to the manuscript. Thank you also goes to my parents Wes and Nancy Fasnacht and sisters Diane and Melanie for their continuing support of all that I set out to accomplish in this life.

Thank you Maegan Sadocha for designing the amazing book covers. You are extremely talented! I have always considered you part of our family. I will be forever grateful to you for catching my vision, not only for this book, but for my Transition Bridges journey.

Wendy Schweifler, thank you for your editing suggestions. You are one of my greatest cheerleaders and promoters. I appreciate you!

A special thank you also goes to my community of readers. You inspire me every day! I appreciate your reactions and comments on my Facebook posts, as well as your encouragement to me on this journey. You are a blessing!

Thank you to the readers of this book. I hope it has inspired you to go out and be a blessing to those around you. Never underestimate the power of creating "taking tea" moments with others. Your one small ripple of kindness may result in a tsunami of blessings for others. We may not know each other, but I am praying for you. Maybe one day we will even share a "take tea" moment together.

Made in the USA
Columbia, SC
08 December 2019